ADDICTED TO
Hash
The man, not the drug

Copyright © 2016 by Zavane

No part of this publication may be reproduced, or transmitted in any form or by any means, electronic, photocopying, recording or otherwise, without the prior written permission of the copyright holder.

ISBN 978-0-947480-11-0

Women are Queens and all of us have encountered Men in our lives and they are the Kings.

They've been our grandfathers, fathers, brothers, uncles, cousins, friends and more ROYALLY our lovers.

This work of spirit is about one such lover.

His spirit was, is and will always be special to mine. We connected like tangle weeds, I'm convinced our spirits recognized each other from another place and time.

We queens know about being tangled, it's the roller coaster ride we never planned on but went on any way.

These writings will take you on that ride. Many of you will feel like you've been on the exact same ride and I'm sure we would agree at times it's been both exhilarating and scary.

All I know is that we Queens know how to represent and that when we decide to get off the ride we all straighten out our outfits fix our hair and adjust our crowns.

As for the king, well the king, he either finds a smoother ride for us both to enjoy or he just gets on another roller coaster, this one being more intense than the last but eventually he finds his way to the castle where his Queen has been waiting patiently.

Much Peace, Love & Respect
To the Kings & Queens

Zavane

She: You're beautiful, let's hook up

He: Would love too but I'm not available until 2017

She: smiles awkwardly

He: And yes, I'd love to hook up then

RESERVATIONS

You won't touch me

But you did

That night when no words were needed

Two souls just longing to connect

A level of euphoric consciousness

A space reserved just for the two of us

A gift

That you're afraid to accept fully

Taking a piece of it periodically

Afraid of your own greatness

Of whom you become

When you enter the space

Reserved just for the two of us

We only scratched the surface

Of the gift in its entirety

Left longing for more, I feel abandoned

I can't go there with anyone else

It was

Reserved just for the two of us

I want to scream "help me"

But I swallow my words

I know you can't enter if you're afraid

You have to want to go

You have to accept the gift graciously

In limbo with only a memory to sustain

I am losing my mind

Want to experience that again

That space

Reserved just for the two of us

Please don't push me in to the arms of another

Don't make me live life with an ordinary lover

Someone who can't enter that space

Reserved just for the two of us

I'll never forget this moment but it is the past,
today I move forward by...

3 NAMES

They say when you name a child it is important to remember that every time they are addressed their spirit is reminded of what is has been called to BE.

He has been called ETERNAL
He will be with me forever
He has been called POWER OF GOD
For me, he is a force so strong unlike any I've ever known
He has been called DESTROYER OF EVIL
I know not evil anymore, He is love in the purest form

The man with three names
Each different
Each affecting me the same
I'll never forget Him
Eternal He will be
I'll never be weak again
I've had the Power of God in me
Thou I may walk through the valley of the shadows of death
I will fear no evil
For He has destroyed it
All that He is and all that He will be
Is all that I will ever need
For me to BE Free

I will/have named my male child with hopes that he will...

AUGUST 2ND
Every year

So today is the day that it's all said and done

The day I accept that you're not the one

Erasing the past from every device

So when the thoughts come, I won't have to think twice

There'll be no more memories, not ones I can see

No starring at pictures, of what used to be

On this day I vow to make a new start

And no, not with you am I leaving my heart

I'm taking it with me

We journey as one

Thought it was your love that I'd be losing

But it's mine that I have won

The day I made this decision, I felt...

CLASSIC *Man*

He's a Classic Man
Or he at least wants to be
Bounded by memories of yesterday
Conflicting with thoughts of you and me
Who currently want to be
A part of his world no matter where that may be
His love is not objective
He loves us all the same
This would be his life if we'd concede
To him it's not a game
To play with the hearts of those who tend to go insane
Waiting for reciprocation from the man who has three names
Let's just call him Classic Man and let's just let him be
The character in the video
The one who has all three
Women, wives, loves
Not objective
Can't you see?
That he must love us all the same and at times
He must leave us be
To try and find another love
Who would make us feel the same
Exhausted from our efforts
We gratefully choose to remain
With The Classic Man
The one who must be free
To love us all the same
However, paradoxically…
You, Her & Me

*If I ever found myself in this situation
I would...*

I'M Complicated

I'm Complicated

Was the warning that he gave

What he meant was;

ISH ain't been easy

Dad left

My Mama turned to stone

I tried my best to raise my brothers

With what little I had been shown

Of course I was never good enough

No matter how hard I tried

So, I just gave up on this thing called love

I've tried and then I've cried

Like buckets of tears because over the years

So many hearts I have broken

The words "I Love You' are so complicated

When to me they are spoken

Love looks different to me

You wouldn't understand

And to add to this ISH

I still gotta be a man

Sons who look up to me

They say I am their hero

My life's filled with things I'd never want them to know

I'm drawn to you but I must pull back

I'm not equipped, there's so much I lack

At times I think I love you in my own twisted way

But I'm complicated and I've got to pull away

Don't say that you'll miss me

Cause that'll mess me up even more

And baby please, please don't cry

Wait til I'm out the door

I just know that I can't love you the way you want me to

I don't even understand why I am drawn to you

Wait...

Could You be love?

Love, could this Be You

I know that I cannot fix him so now I must...

DISOBEDIENT

I did the one thing he had asked me not to do

I called

The number he had called me from many times

The same one I committed to memory after he disconnected his mobile

I called because I missed him

Hadn't heard from him in a while

Well, ok it was just the weekend

But, still I felt justified in calling him

I lied and said that my name was Karen

Who the fcuk was she anyways?

Probably another member of his harem

So, I didn't care that it might ruin his connect

Label me disobedient, have him lose all respect

For me

In that moment I needed more than he would ever know

Wanted to feel the love that he would never show

To me

So,

To me and for me I've fcuked it all up

By doing the one thing he had asked me not to

Oh well, what's a girl to do?

Just then 3 little birds sat on my doorstep

Told me not to worry bout a thing

Especially not my damn mobile going ring, ring, ring

I've done something I had been asked not to and it has left me...

I SLIPPED
& Fell

He was there for me when you were, well, just too busy

I thought he could help me to understand you better

But he took the focus off of you

And placed it on me

Showed me my worth

Listened to me venting about all the things you wouldn't do

Then reminded me I was of value…valuable

He never tired of telling me how much I was worth

I liked what he was saying

It changed my perspective

From you to me from hurt to hope

I liked what he was saying

It inspired me to be better

He said "don't give your energy to someone who doesn't give you theirs"

He was giving me his energy

So I guess it only made sense

That

I

Fell

For

Your

Best friend

Hmmm, now how exactly would I handle this?...

HE DOESN'T FEEL *Free*

He doesn't feel free
Can't be him self when he's with me
Strong vibes infused with love
Love, it's all she knows how to be
She chooses to forget the other vibes
The ones infused with hurt, anger and hate
She knows that as long as she has life
It's not too late
So her love scares him and pushes him away
But her love, also infused with patience
Allows her to wait
Because pretending she feels any differently
Isn't something she can do
As she questions; why can't I be me and you be you?
She is presented two options
Love him as you do and walk away
Pretend that you don't and get to spend another day
With the greatest pretender of the two
As he's great at pretending that he doesn't love you

I love him but I don't have time for games.
I'm...

PLACEHOLDER

He expresses interest
With actions that validate his words
He's consistent
"Good morning, have a great day!"
"Hey, how's your day going?'
"How was your day, you good?"
Questions I am happy to answer
Conversations that last all night
Have us both oversleeping
Getting to know each other intimately
No bodily fluids shared, not yet
He wants to know where this is going
Exactly where we're at
I exhale as I smile and think of you
And the very first time we met
And as I look at him and think of you
I know I cannot tell him, that
He's just a placeholder
And I really want to be with you
The one with all the right words but no action
The one as inconsistent as March weather
The one whose bodily fluids I crave
The one who leaves me feeling like I've been blindfolded and left in a maze
Should I move your setting over or just simply pack it away
To make space
For him
The one who wants to stay

In this moment I choose to be happy and with that choice I choose...

HOPELESS
Hope

He gives her a hope unheard of

And ill will has never been his intention

He just likes to share sometimes

With someone he knows will care

Someone he can trust

Someone with whom there's no must

He doesn't mean to hurt her

Or anyone for that matter

He just likes to share sometimes

You know, be himself without reservation

With someone he knows will care

He shares and he is satisfied

Not knowing another part of her has died

It was never his intention to cause her any affliction

He just likes to share sometimes

With someone he knows will care

She cares deeply and intently but never says a word

She allows him to share his soul

Her voice is seldom heard

With tears in her eyes and a ponding heart

She allows him to share his soul

And every time she starts

She hesitates and allows him to share some more

She berates herself after for not saying what she feels

But somehow it always feels right

To allow another layer to peel

To give him more and to take her less

She somehow feels that this is best

To love him from the other end

And allow his heart to mend

By sharing whatever's in that moment

She feels his love for her

And when that moment is over

And the sharing comes to an end

She begins the never ending process

Of allowing her heart to mend

Until

Next time

I've been his sounding board for a long time,
it's now time for me to...

I AM A
Queen

I'm an angry black woman

That's what he said

I be rolling my eyes

And shaking my head

Moving with attitude

Behavior not exhibited by a queen

I'm just fcuking angry and downright mean

I'm not angry I say

And if I am at times, it's you who made me this way

It's more like hurt

I say and look away

Can't let him see my eyes

Because they'd tell all

They'd show that his words hurt like hell

And made me feel real small

As I compose myself and turn to walk away

I think these words I know I'll never say

I am a queen and you had me

I loved you like no other

I sacrificed and toiled

Never expecting much

Let alone to be spoiled

I am a queen, yes, I mean me!

It was you my love

The king who wouldn't be

His shortcomings are not a reflection of who I know I am.
No matter his perception I will...

REFLECTIONS

I believed him
Every word he said
Even when his actions conflicted
He left
I healed
He came back
Said she meant nothing
Just a business partner
I believed him
Every word he said
He came back
And this time I feel real pain
Cause now he's gone away again
Consciously I chose for him to stay
Sub consciously I did things so he would go away
Conscious reflects on what is
Sub conscious on what was
Conscious said he's here now
Sub said he'll leave again
Sub was right, he left but now there's no more pain
Never again will I diss the sub believing just because…
I want to
I love him, I always will
But now I know what I have to do

Love you brother from a distance
Ain't no getting through to you
That this is not a game
And my heart is not the pond
Cause a sister's love goes deep
To the stars, sun moon and beyond
Take your trifling game to the tables
Hope you'll find someone to play
Take it anywhere you want to
Just never come back this way
Cause sub is my reminder
Ensures I never forget
That it's all a fcuking illusion
Even tho you're right in front of me
That you cannot be what you don't know
And I, I can only be me
And who and what I am is love
It's all there, just look into my eyes
But you can't and you won't because you know
That you'll finally realize
That no matter how many games you play
You've already lost this prize

I know that I'm done because...

I DECLARE THAT
the possibility that who I am is
THE STAND I TAKE

The stand I take is:

I am the creator of my life.

I am powerful and worthy

I am enough

I am unlimited access to infinite possibilities

I am choice and I trust myself fully

I am love

And I support people with understanding and compassion

I am my word

Zavane

*If your word is your bond, what would you declare,
what stand would you take for you?*

LADIES HAVE YOU EVER
had a man who just disappears?

You know what I mean right? Like one of my friends is living with dude and every two weeks or so he goes missing, like to his crib for a few days to a week. Now ain't that just the strangest ish ever??

So let me tell you bout the love of my life.

Yeah, love of my life, Casper the friendly fcuking ghost!

Dude would love me then leave me for like a month at a time

Then he would return as if everything was fine

I was so damn happy to see him that I never complained

Until that damn man up and left again

Ish got a little bit better a month became two weeks

But hell, 24 hours is long when outside love is what you seek

So this one time when he went away for about 3 months

And I had nothing but time

I began the journey to look inside and was so surprised to find

The love I had for me was true

No leaving when the rent was due or when it needed space

It was there with me-my ride or die

No thing or man could ever replace

The love that I own it belongs to me

No if or buts, no maybes

Never could I have imagined

That this was how it could be

So Casper's gone away again and this time I don't care

Cause the love I have for myself

Doesn't require that he be here

So ladies take some time to find that love

The one that's pure and true

That love that's rare and irreplaceable

The love that's inside of you

And trust when dude comes back this time

He's gonna have to represent

And love me

Like I do

I show I love myself by...

NO THING

Up past midnight
Drinking wine
Smoking a ciggy
Can't sleep
Thunder and lightening
Vicious rain
It all sounds horrible
Can't quell my thoughts
They keep going to you
No matter how hard I try
Another direction eludes me
It's amazing to know
That if you were here
Just how quick my perspective
On these conditions would change

I just know
That I would think it all so beautiful
I would be secure
I would feel it all so differently
The powers of the elements have
No Thing on me
When I'm with you
They're all so amazingly beautiful
As they were meant to be

What things could you find beautiful if you were home alone in the midst of a storm?...

EVERYWHERE
& Nowhere

He'll give me what I want as long as I don't ask

Not that he thinks I don't deserve it

But fulfilling is a task he doesn't want to perform

Because that'll mean he conforms

And he does that for no one

Acts like he's the only begotten son

And in that belief he'll be like no one

Who you've ever encountered

And still you won't forget the one who wants to be forgettable

Who comes and goes as he so pleases

Ever so playfully and quite knowingly he teases

You

Into succumbing to his wiles and way of being

And with the certainty of the master he'll say none of it had any meaning

He'll say he's everywhere and nowhere

A spirit free to roam

To all corners of the world

With no specific place to call home

Won't be contained in a bubble

Absolutely no fcuking way

"Yo, take me like I am man or I'll check you some other day

Can't be confined to traditions or worry bout how you feel

This life is mine to love and live

And my fate, only I can seal

I love you when I'm with you

Don't miss me when I'm not

Try and understand me woman

Who I am is what you've got

There's no faking or any lies

I'm everywhere and nowhere

I'm even in the skies

The ones you see everyday

Just look up baby

Cause I'm never far away."

Traditional commitments aren't his thing.
I choose to...

SEPTEMBER 17, 2015

He: are you clean yet?

Me: umm, what exactly are you talking about?

He: (smiling) you know exactly what I'm talking about. I'm talking bout my friend…ya him! So, are you?

Me: Ah, that's a long story, a book even. But, YES I AM!

www.ingramcontent.com/pod-product-compliance
Lightning Source LLC
Chambersburg PA
CBHW030226170426
43194CB00007BA/880